by LaShonda M. Stewart
illustrations by JL Straw
designed by Cartoon Studios

For My Late Grandmothers, Beulah Mae Walls and Otha Lee Stewart

I would like to thank my family and friends for their thoughtful insight and suggestions. Their kindness is heartfelt and greatly appreciated.
-LaShonda

by LaShonda M. Stewart
illustrations by JL Straw
designed by Cartoon Studios

Text and illustrations copyright 2020 by LaShonda M. Stewart

All rights reserved. No parts of this publication may be reproduced, or stored in retrieval, or transmitted in any form or by any means, electronic, mechanical, photocopying, recording, or otherwise, without permission of the publisher. For information regarding permission, write to Lee Beau Publishing, 730 Avignon Drive, Suite 103, Ridgeland, Mississippi 39157.

Published in the United States by
Lee Beau Publishing, Jackson, Mississippi.

First Edition

Hardcover ISBN: 9781735602301
Paperback ISBN: 9781735602318

12DaysOfASoulFoodChristmas.com

730 Avignon Dr. Suite 103
Ridgeland, Mississippi 39157

LeeBeauPublishing.com

As Big Mama stands on the front porch with open arms to welcome her grandchildren, the kids yell with excitement as they run towards her.

While cooking, Big Mama starts to hum her favorite song, "The 12 Days of a Soul Food Christmas," and the grandchildren begin to sing along as she prepares for each day.

On the First day of Christmas,
Big Mama gave to me:
a big pot of Black-Eyed Peas.

On the Second day of Christmas,
Big Mama gave to me:
Two Pig's Feet
and a big pot of Black-Eyed Peas.

On the Third day of Christmas,
Big Mama gave to me:
Three Ham Hocks,
Two Pig's Feet
and a big pot of Black-Eyed Peas.

On the Fourth day of Christmas,
Big Mama gave to me:
Four Turkey Necks,
Three Ham Hocks, Two Pig's Feet
and a big pot of Black-Eyed Peas

On the Fifth day of Christmas,
Big Mama gave to me:
FIVE CHICKEN WINGS!!!!
Four Turkey Necks, Three Ham Hocks, Two Pig's Feet
and a big pot of Black-Eyed Peas.

On the Sixth day of Christmas,
Big Mama gave to me:
Six Jugs of Kool-Aid,
FIVE CHICKEN WINGS!!!!
Four Turkey Necks, Three Ham Hocks,
Two Pig's Feet
and a big pot of Black-Eyed Peas.

On the Seventh day of Christmas,
Big Mama gave to me:
Seven Pots of Okra,
Six Jugs of Kool-Aid,
FIVE CHICKEN WINGS!!!!
Four Turkey Necks, Three Ham Hocks,
Two Pig's Feet and a big pot
of Black-Eyed Peas.

On the Eighth day of Christmas,
Big Mama gave to me:
Eight Apple Pies,
Seven Pots of Okra,
Six Jugs of Kool-Aid,
FIVE CHICKEN WINGS!!!!
Four Turkey Necks, Three Ham Hocks,
Two Pig's Feet and a big pot
of Black-Eyed Peas.

On the Ninth Day of Christmas,
Big Mama gave to me:
Nine Pans of Dressing,
Eight Apple Pies,
Seven Pots of Okra,
Six Jugs of Kool-Aid
FIVE CHICKEN WINGS!!!!
Four Turkey Necks, Three Ham Hocks,
Two Pig's Feet and a big pot
of Black-Eyed Peas

On the Tenth day of Christmas,
Big Mama gave to me:
Ten Big Ole Turkeys,

Nine Pans of Dressing,
Eight Apple Pies,
Seven Pots of Okra,
Six Jugs of Kool-Aid,
FIVE CHICKEN WINGS!!!!
Four Turkey Necks, Three Ham Hocks,
Two Pig's Feet and a big pot
of Black-Eyed Peas.

On the Eleventh Day of Christmas,
Big Mama gave to me:
Eleven Pans of Cornbread,

Ten Big Ole Turkeys.
Nine Pans of Dressing,
Eight Apple Pies,
Seven Pots of Okra,
Six Jugs of Kool-Aid,
FIVE CHICKEN WINGS!!!!
Four Turkey Necks, Three Ham Hocks,
Two Pig's Feet and a big pot
of Black-Eyed Peas.

On the Twelfth Day of Christmas, Big Mama gave to me:

Twelve Pots of Chit'lins,
Eleven Pans of Cornbread,
Ten Big Ole Turkeys!!!
Nine Pans of Dressing, Eight Apple Pies,
Seven Pots of Okra, Six Jugs of Kool-Aid,
FIVE CHICKEN WINGS!!!!
Four Turkey Necks, Three Ham Hocks,
Two Pig's Feet and a big pot
of Black-Eyed Peas!!!

The End!

LaShonda M. Stewart, PhD, is a Professor at Southern Illinois University and teaches in the Master of Public Administration Program in the School of Management and Marketing at Southern Illinois University in Carbondale. She teaches and researches in the area of public budgeting and financial management and has publications appearing in journals such as Public Budgeting and Finance, Journal of Public Budgeting, Accounting & Financial Management, and Administration & Society. The author also expresses her creativity by writing children's books and giving motivational speeches. She can be reached at lms10@siu.edu.

JL Straw is an illustrator and comic book artist based in the United Kingdom. JL Straw has had a passion and love for illustrating throughout her entire life. She actually got her professional start by drawing comics, shortly therafter specializing in the craft of inking as well as enjoying a five-year career in editing children's educational comic books. Recently she has turned her drawing expertise and storytelling skill into illustrating children's books with this being her debut in the children's book industry.

LeeBeauPublishing.com

Printed in the USA
CPSIA information can be obtained
at www.ICGtesting.com
LVHW070323191023
761326LV00014B/195